WICKED WILLIE'S LOW-DOWN ON MEN

The essential guide to male misbehaviour

Cartoons and captions by Gray Jolliffe
Text by Peter Mayle

Pan Books
London and Sydney

First published 1987 by Pan Books Ltd,
Cavaye Place, London SW10 9PG
9 8 7 6 5 4 3 2 1
Cartoons and Wicked Willie character © Gray Jolliffe 1987
Text © Peter Mayle 1987

ISBN 0 330 30137 3

Printed and bound in Spain by
Mateu Cromo Artes Graphica, SA, Madrid

THE COOLIDGE SYNDROME:

Mrs. Coolidge, wife of the famous American president, was on a guided tour of a Massachusetts dairy farm.

"Tell me," she asked, "How many times a day does the average rooster perform"?

"About twelve times," was the reply.

"Tell that to the president," said Mrs Coolidge.

When the president was told, he was a little dismayed. Then a thought occurred to him.

"Does the rooster always perform with the same hen"? he asked.

"No, always a different hen," they said.

"Tell that to Mrs Coolidge", said the president.

THE LATEST SCORE

In case anyone should doubt the serious nature of the subject under discussion in the pages which follow, it is necessary to start with a statistic:

40,000,000 BC: world population = 2

1987: world population = 5,000,000,000

What has happened to turn the world from a nice empty place where you could always find a parking spot into the overcrowded chaos it is today? Improved medical techniques? A high-fibre diet? Computerized dating services? No.

It is the behaviour of man, or rather his misbehaviour, which has systematically done the damage, clogged up the wide open spaces and added several hundred yards to the length of the checkout queue at the supermarket. And who is the driving force behind this compulsion to go forth and multiply? The dreadful little mathematical wizard himself, ready at the drop of a hat, or indeed any article of clothing, to stand up and be counted.

Well-informed sources put the proportion of men in the world as high as fifty per cent, and it is little short of astonishing that an anti-social group of this size hasn't been exposed and locked up by now. But the fact is that men are still behaving badly, and women are still falling for it.

Some optimist (a man, naturally) said that 'To understand is to forgive'. Hence this guide, which offers no excuses but one or two explanations.

RAMPANT YOUTH

We have often been told that life is unfair, and that youth is wasted on the young. The truth of both statements is obvious when we consider the agonizing predicament of anyone in the first flush of manhood.

Youth is the one time in a man's life when Willie and his owner are completely agreed about priority number one: to find a nubile young lovely and jump on her with cries of joy. Days and nights are spent in wishful thinking. The female form is studied with the kind of yearning intensity that politicians go through when looking at Number 10 Downing Street, and with more or less the same thought in mind: *If only I could get in there*.

Physically, you and Willie are at your peak, since we're told that it's all downhill after eighteen. You have nothing to distract you in the way of second mortgages, corporate takeovers or finding the school fees. You are in a perfect position to be passion's plaything and a dedicated researcher into the divine mystery of womanhood. Only three obstacles stand between you and bliss:

1 You're broke.
2 All you have is a bicycle, and with the best will in the world it's difficult to be romantic on a crossbar.
3 The girls you like are, for unaccountable reasons, infatuated with ancient creeps who must be twenty-five if they're a day.

Hey, we've got a date with Marcie today!
So just don't blow it okay?
Hi Marcie! Shall we play hide the sausage?
He blew it!

When you wake up each morning with these unpleasant facts (not to mention Willie) staring you in the face, it doesn't take long before a major Formative Influence begins to make itself felt. Doctors call this frustration, and it can lead to acne, an interest in football and several other unsavoury side effects which we needn't go into here.

It is during these uncomfortable times that certain characteristics can develop in male behaviour which often last throughout adult life. For instance:

Group leering

When three or more men are gathered together in a mixed social situation, they will often perform this primitive ritual. Keeping at a safe distance from the object of their attentions – the girl on the corner whose sweater is one size too small – they will take it in turns to cast sultry glances in her direction, followed by muttered comments, winks, nudges and general hilarity. If the brazen hussy should have the nerve to approach them, they will stop laughing and talk about snooker, because the whole point about the group leer is that it is a complete pastime in itself, an example of male bonding that collapses when its bluff is called.

Rose-coloured hindsight

It is strange and wonderful how the memory, given enough encouragement, can turn rejection and disaster into a form of triumph. Let us suppose that your timid advances have been laughingly dismissed. Or, worse still, that they have been encouraged, but due to flaws in your technique and gaps in your knowledge the episode has ended in embarrassment. The rational side of you has to admit that you put up a totally inept performance. Willie, on the other hand, whose ego is out of all proportion to his size and who cannot conceive of blame or failure, will gradually persuade you that it was *her* fault. She was obviously terrified of unleashing the full force of your virility, and will now have to go through life not knowing what she missed.

Success by innuendo

This is a highly skilled art which has been known to give many a mouse the reputation of a lion. It consists of dropping vague but infinitely suggestive hints about young ladies who are known to you and your friends. Gentlemanly discretion prevents you from reporting all the lurid details, but the inference is that you have gone where none of your friends has been able to go. Delivered with enough confidence, and to a gullible audience, the virgin thus becomes Casanova without once having taken off his trousers in earnest. In later life, men who are unusually gifted in this use of innuendo can make a good living as gossip columnists.

The sympathetic slander

Used as a last resort, when rejection has been too public to ignore or deny and everyone knows you got absolutely nowhere. Naturally, it couldn't have been because of your lack of charm or ability, so what was it? You take the questioner into your confidence and, generous spirit that you are, tell him that you feel really sorry for the girl: she's got a terrible problem. *She doesn't like men*. Many innocent girls and women have been classified as freaks in this way, but Willie couldn't care less. His pride is undented. All these disgraceful tactics are not merely tolerated by other men, but actively encouraged – on the basis that you never know when you might need to use one of them yourself.

Before we go any further there's something you should know. I'm a CONDOMS carrier

It is part of belonging to an enormous international club which has always excused bad behaviour and closed ranks at the first sign of trouble. Membership is men only. And the club motto – which could have been dictated by Willie himself – is Boys Will Be Boys.

THE YEARS OF INDISCRETION

Ever since our old friend prehistoric man crept guiltily back to the family cave with a telltale smudge of woad on his hairy cheek and a slightly dented club, the world has been full of masculine mischief. And despite occasional deterrents, like late-night television, things seem to be getting worse rather than better – particularly when man reaches those golden years of commonsense and maturity which come in between hot-blooded youth and harmless dotage.

Students of sociology are always trying to explain why it is that men who are old enough to know better are constantly being caught, figuratively, and sometimes literally, with their trousers down. No section of society is immune: cabinet ministers and vicars, plumbers and milkmen, schoolmasters and long-distance lorry drivers – they're all at it, providing the *News of the Screws* with endless material. The explanations put forward by learned observers for this continuing phenomenon vary from a desperate attempt to recapture the joys of young manhood to a charitable urge to take wayward girls in hand, but these are merely symptoms of a more fundamental conflict.

A TERRIBLE MISUNDERSTANDING:

What in God's name are you doing??

I think I'm going to put in for a transfer...

It is, of course, the enemy below who should be exposed as the motivating factor. He it is who points the way to catastrophe, whether it takes the form of a love-nest in Fulham, a sudden interest in nature rambles, or a torrid interlude behind the filing cabinets during the office party. When a man stops going to the pub and starts attending art classes (this term's subject: the reclining nude), it's not hard to guess who's at the bottom of it.

By now, Wicked Willie's role as wrecker of promising careers and spanner in the matrimonial works is well known. He has popped up throughout recorded history, exerting a degree of influence on events which,

considering his modest size and deplorable personality, is quite remarkable. But why is it that he achieves his most spectacular triumphs during the years of maturity, when one would expect man's wisdom and experience to be more than a match for Willie's worst efforts?

The truth will now be told. Like many a breakthrough in human knowledge and understanding, this one is basically very simple; with the help of some courageously explicit diagrams, we can now put our finger on the crux of man's most enduring problem.

PHILOSOPHY

We're meeting Wendy. She's a virgin
I've heard it's curable
With her, not a hope.
Still, I s'pose a blow-job will be better than nothing

THE PETER PAN THEORY

Anatomical drawings like these have never before graced the pages of any textbook.

Figure 1 shows man at the age of seventeen, and Wicked Willie, also at the age of seventeen. Note the similiarities between the two: ruddy complexions, sprightly posture, a generally optimistic cast to both countenances. They might almost be brothers, so pronounced is the resemblance between the two.

However, in **Figure 2**, after a few years, some disturbing changes have taken place. One member of our fresh-faced couple is looking distinctly the worse for wear.

Figure 3 shows man and Wicked Willie many years later. It reveals with hideous clarity what the experts have overlooked.

As you see, man has changed his shape, lost his hair, developed a furrowed brow, bloodshot eyes and fallen arches. *But Willie is exactly as he was at seventeen*. He hasn't put on an ounce. His hairline hasn't receded. He still regards the world with a bright and optimisitic eye. He is unmarked by the passage of time. (Wrinkles don't count; he was always prematurely wrinkled.)

Alas for us all, the little brute seems to be ageless. While we may suffer from stress, high blood pressure, slipped discs and slipped chests, Willie continues to enjoy rude health and a boyish enthusiasm for all that life and love have to offer. He is the permanent teenager, a small but vibrant example of eternal youth, constantly on the lookout for someone to play with.

And he is seldom disappointed, because the years of maturity bring with them increased social opportunities, more travel, more money and a heightened appreciation of the fair sex. In other words, the chances of getting into trouble are vastly greater than they were in younger and less prosperous days. As we shall see.

SEX EDUCATION ON TV

Good Heavens! 80% of married men cheat in this country
Yeah?..
So where do the rest of them cheat?

CONTRACEPTION FOR MEN

Vasectomy is not reversible but nowadays the more sophisticated condoms are. Tweed on one side and navy pin-stripe on the other depending on whether you're in town or week-ending. Vasectomy is now unpopular because it doesn't give you this kind of choice. It can also be quite dangerous:

HIGH-RISK SITUATIONS AND EROGENOUS ZONES

There are two elements which combine, when man is in the prime of life, to put the seal of disaster on any plans for respectability.

The first is a realization that, contrary to the old cliché, flattery will actually get you quite a long way. No longer a shy or tongue-tied youth, mature man is at his most plausible, and finds that a good line in sympathetic small-talk can often be more effective with the ladies than a passing resemblance to Robert Redford. We have all seen young and beautiful girls at parties apparently fascinated by the most plain and uninspiring of men: overweight, badly dressed, and probably with at least one wife and several children tucked away in Croydon, there he is, monopolizing the attentions of this ravishing creature – and she seems to be loving it. Can it be that they share an obsessive interest in gardening? Is he perhaps an Italian prince travelling incognito? Far from it. He is just a man who has discovered that the tongue is mightier than a handsome profile. And giving all the immoral support he can is his partner in crime, the unseen guest.

The second benefit that comes with time is a dramatic increase in pocket money. Banks and credit card companies obviously feel that your youthful follies are now over, and that you have reached the age of the safe bet. Consequently they fall over themselves in their haste to provide overdrafts, gold cards and lines of credit which stretch to infinity (or death, which ever comes first). In theory, these extra funds should be put to some prudent use like double glazing the family home or investing in the Channel tunnel. In practice, Wicked Willie takes over as financial director and blows the lot on intimate dinners

used to hold sports days.

Short of making a drastic career move and becoming a monk, there is little that can be done to avoid temptation. No set of circumstances which involves both sexes is entirely safe, and some occasions are almost guaranteed to end in tears, or alimony, or both. And it's no use deluding yourself that being forewarned will keep you out of trouble; it never has in the past. The only advantage of knowing in advance what fate has in store is that you have a little longer to invent your excuses.

However, even that small help is better than

ONAN'S LAW

If you play with anything long enough it breaks.

and weekends in Paris. But then he's not responsible for the interest payments.

Looked at in this detached and scientific manner, it is obvious that man is fighting a losing battle. He has a persuasive line in chat, credit burning a hole in his pocket, and a constant companion in his trousers with a mental age of seventeen. It is a recipe for fun and games unmatched since the times when nudist colonies

nothing, and it is with this in mind that we offer a representative selection of the most common pitfalls.

These are not put forward as unproved and hypothetical possibilities. They have been field tested by men all over the world for generations. The fact that they are still as dangerous as ever is a tribute to Willie's vigorous refusal to act his age.

I'm in love with that Janie
Me too!
She's the perfect wife for you
But she's already married
Perfect!

Other people's weddings

There is something about weddings which brings out the beast in otherwise well-behaved men. Love is in the air – or if not love, a mixture of alcohol and bridesmaids that goes straight to Willie's head. Matters are made even worse by the appearance and behaviour of the female guests, because women at weddings are usually dressed in their best, and have applied the Chanel No. 5 with a liberal hand. They are also inclined to drink a little more than usual, and as a result become skittish, flirtatious and ready to laugh at off-colour jokes about beds and honeymoons. And as a final threat to social equilibrium, there is always a fair chance of bumping into an Old Flame, looking younger and more attractive with every glass of champagne.

Against this joyous background events unfold with the inevitability of a Greek tragedy. As the drink takes over and Willie shifts into high gear, we see a display of leering and lurching and thigh-squeezing, of illicit kisses snatched behind the floral arrangement, of dishevelled couples emerging after a hectic half hour in the cloakroom, of telephone numbers being scrawled in lipstick on napkins – in other words, enough activity to make sure that the trip home in the car for most couples takes place in an atmosphere of icy recrimination.

The third passenger, however, has had a wonderful time. He has also memorized the phone number of the blonde who kept trying to dance on the table. Willie likes weddings.

Business trips to Los Angeles

Even looked at on a statistical basis, the odds in Los Angeles are overwhelmingly stacked against the businessman who is trying to behave himself. There are, so we're told, seventeen unattached women roaming the streets for every man – a ratio which accounts for the lethargic bearing of the male residents. They're not laid back, poor devils. They're exhausted.

But the statistics tell only half the story. What makes Los Angeles the closest thing Wicked Willie will ever find to a spiritual home is that **a)** the female natives are very friendly, and **b)** they all seem to be Willie's age – that is, a well-developed seventeen, with a keen interest in sunbathing and wearing as few clothes as possible. And if by chance you should ever let slip that you have connections in the movie business, you run a serious risk of being seized and wrestled to the ground by a hopeful starlet looking for a part. (Willie, needless to say, will put his own interpretation on this.)

There is only one certain way to avoid getting into trouble in LA, and that is to do all your business over the phone from Chicago.
Local dialect note: When faced with a problem, the young ladies of Los Angeles will often say, 'It's no biggie'. Don't take it personally.

Controlled studies have shown that the probability of meeting Miss Perfect increases by a factor of ten when you:
a) Are with your wife
b) Are with a more attractive male friend
c) Have had garlic for lunch

Fame

Men may choose to regard fame as the public recognition of their brilliant talents. Willie knows better: fame is an aphrodisiac more potent than looks or money, capable of overcoming primitive manners and a lack of personal hygiene (one or two artistic personalities spring to mind here, but on legal advice they must remain evil smelling and nameless).

What else but fame can explain the highly publicized 'friendships' between statuesque beauties and gentlemen who seem perfectly cast by nature to be models for garden gnomes or second-hand car salesmen? Money comes into it, certainly, but the prime attraction is fame.

Rubbing shoulders with well-known men leads, more often than not, to more intimate contact. From there it's a short step to wearing oversized sunglasses at Heathrow, pretending to be outraged when photographers catch you coming out of restaurants, and all the rest of it.

Willie is in his element. The time he considers wasted – that is, the period between formal introduction and nudity – is reduced to a minimum. His whims are excused. Each time he performs, it is to an admiring audience. If he decides not to appear, he is forgiven. One way and another, being attached to someone famous is Willie's idea of heaven.

At the weekend let's find a cottage near a quiet beach and romp naked in the waves..

... So don't forget your CONDOMS..

It isn't necessary to be world famous, either. A single exposure on the Terry Wogan Show has been known to do the trick. And as final disturbing evidence of the link between modest fame and immodest goings-on, just think how many politicians have been caught with their manifestos showing. Is it because, despite their safe seats, they are devils in the boudoir? Not likely. It's because they are, in their own small way, famous.

As it says on page one of *The Thoughts of Wicked Willie*: 'Show me a famous man and I'll show you a good time.'

New Year's Eve

Of all the events in the social calendar that can be classified as risky, New Year's Eve is far and away the most dangerous. Every year, millions of men wake up on the first of January and wish they hadn't, so ominous are the memories that come flooding back. Did you really offer to drink champagne out of someone's brassière? Was it you crawling around under the table conducting your own private Most Beautiful Knees contest? Yes, it probably was.

The terrible thing about New Year's Eve is that the whole structure of the evening leads inevitably to a state of social chaos. From the moment everyone puts on those ridiculous paper hats, normal inhibitions disappear. As midnight approaches, Willie consults his watch and prepares to make his move. This is the one night of the year when indecent assault is not only tolerated, but expected, and he's been under starter's orders for hours, jockeying for position so that as the clock strikes twelve he is handily placed to pounce on the little brunette with the big balloons. Happy New Year! Willie, for one, is not going to let old acquaintance be forgot, and if he can manage a couple of new acquaintances as well, so much the better.

Where am I? Who are you??
You got hopelessly drunk last night and the worst possible thing happened
What?
Nothing

MATURITY

The majority of men don't live long enough to reach a recognisable state of mental maturity, though experience teaches most of them to fake it. Sometimes they even fool themselves.

e.g.

IMMATURE

POLITICS
The one thing we in the West should value above all else is our freedom ...
Specially when you've been thrown inside as often as I have.

Now there's a beautiful young couple..
Made in Heaven!
Ask them if they'd like a foursome

The office party

According to a piece of research commissioned by the Extra-Curricular Activities Committee attached to the Institute of Directors, more discarded underwear is found in office waste-paper baskets during December than during the other eleven months put together. The Committee, men to a man, have tried to keep this quiet, because it shows all too clearly what really goes on when captains of industry reward their loyal staff with a little office party.

Management executives will always tell you that it is an important aspect of happy staff relations – a rare chance to have a long chat with old Joe in the accounts department. As it happens, old Joe will be lucky to get three minutes and a glass of warm sherry, since the true purpose of the office party is to find out if Miss Palmer in claim adjustments is as much fun as her saucy manner and five-inch heels suggest.

And so, for this one magical night, new meaning is given to some dusty old official phrases: 'Come into my office and take something down' is the most popular, closely followed by invitations to see the sales curve, or a really original piece of display material, or a new line in Christmas bonuses. A good time is had by all, especially Willie, and there can be no doubt that these occasions help enormously in bringing the staff closer together. There may be a nasty moment when displays of comradeship are overheard taking place on the couch in the Chairman's office, but this can usually be stopped by a strongly worded memo slid under the door.

Medium-risk situations

Not quite as fraught with peril as the old favourites, but claiming victims every day are:

- Unisex hairdressing salons
- Au pair girls in need of tuition in English
- Dimly lit bars
- Secretaries with vital statistics which exceed their typing speeds
- Motels on the A303

- Tennis lessons
- Experiments with home video cameras
- Multiple occupancy jacuzzis

(For men determined to keep out of trouble, here is a small selection of low-risk situations: pony-trekking in Albania, Disneyland, single-handed yacht racing and most of Grimsby.)

Meaning what?
Your friend John is horribly promiscuous.
He's getting more than I am!

MAN'S OTHER BEST FRIEND: THE PHONE

The great advantage of the phone is that it lets a man get away with murder, always providing he can keep a straight voice and thus prevent the caller from guessing what's really going on. As in:

'Honestly, there's nothing I'd like better than dinner with your parents, but something's just come up at work.'

'You're *what*? Are you sure? How wonderful!'

'I can't talk now. You know what these sales conferences are like.'

'Of course I love you.'

'It's a real drag, but I have to take that big American client out.'

'Oh, hi. I've been trying to call you for days. Are you sure your phone's working?'

PHYSICS:

When a body is immersed in water the telephone rings

'This is a terrible line. I can hardly hear you.'

'*Who* called? I've never heard of her.'

'You're not going to believe this, but . . . '

'I know I promised, but you should see what's landed in my in-tray.'

Here's a weird perversion we've never tried - Celibacy!
Not with me you dont!
SEX FOR OLD HANDS

Boy, you must have been really bad in your last life
I mean - I can't imagine a worse punishment...
Than discovering your owner is GAY!
Tinklepoo! Gay willies adore being gay or they'd go on strike!
Come on - we're off to see Bruce!
Oh, whoopee!!

Dunno about you Marge, but at moments like this I come dangerously close to saying 'to Hell with our platonic relationship.'
So it would appear

MEN AND THEIR FUNNY LITTLE WAYS

Try as they might to be otherwise, men are not usually very successful at concealing their amorous adventures. Small but significant changes take place in the behavioural pattern of the man who, prompted by his youthful companion, is up to no good. We have all observed these signs in others (never ourselves), but operating on the Boys Will Be Boys principle, we pretend not to notice them.

Nevertheless, when Wicked Willie is getting the upper hand in daily life, the effects on a man's conduct and appearance are immediately apparent to those who know what to look for, such as a reasonably sharp-eyed secretary. Wives always complain that they are the last to find out, but that's understandable because the errant husband is rarely home; he's at the office. Or so he says.

The most obvious giveaways, in no particular order, are as follows:

A new aftershave

Gone is the brisk and hearty scent of pine needles or bay rum. In its place we find a sultry concoction which, according to the advertisements, practically guarantees a girl with every bottle, and has an effective range of about twenty feet.

A new wardrobe

More flattering suits, more colourful ties and – the final hopeful touch – a complete reassessment in the underwear department. No more tired, grey Y-fronts, but a collection of masculine lingerie that would put an embroidered Renaissance codpiece to shame. Willie knows that his chances are greatly increased if his appendage – i.e. you – is as attractively turned out as possible, even down to the most intimate garments.

A new haircut

We are assuming here that there is enough hair left to cut. Men with a fine head of skin sometimes resort to face fur – moustaches, beards or those bushy sideburns so much admired in Victorian times.

A sudden interest in fitness

The recent proliferation of gyms and workout parlours is a direct result of Willie's insistence that the middle-aged spread be removed to permit greater agility and closer contact. All this talk about improving the cardiovascular system is a smokescreen.

A more attentive attitude to the nearest and dearest

When a man starts sending his family off on holidays – without him, due to pressure of work – it is not because he wants to catch up on his filing.

A new hobby

And it won't be fishing or carpentry.

THE MALE MENOPAUSE

This is something that only happens to other men, but there do seem to be a lot of them about.

Their distinguishing characteristics are a refusal to accept that they have outgrown their trousers, that sudden movements on the dance floor are likely to end in traction, or that nineteen-year-old girls are immune to their charm and *savoir-faire*.

It is during this period that men are driven to try various rejuvenation techniques, such as monkey glands, vividly coloured knee-length dressing gowns, and Porsches (despite the fact that these are as difficult to get into as their trousers). As one might expect, Willie is not the sort to take a minor problem like menopause lying down, although occasionally he has to, due to his owner's tendency to fall asleep at inappropriate moments.

Trying times indeed, and who can say how long they will last? All we know is that they do eventually come to an end, ushering in the golden era of the Dirty Old Man.

THE MALE MENOPAUSE

The male menopause is a very real condition causing the loss of many millions of man hours each day, particularly in big cities where there are plenty of girls.

At a certain age some men worry about the loss of their youth and start acting strange..

TOTAL FILTH FOR ADULTS

...like going to a trendy hair dresser..

Shall I dress both of them, love?

.. and chasing young women.

I'd love to get to know you better but how about a spot of dinner first?

Suddenly they try to get in shape...

Try to memorise the top ten...
Get new clothes... Get an old sports car...

Boogie till the small hours...

Conclusion: The male menopause is no bad thing so long as you have credit cards to help you through.

OLD AGE

By now Willie is beginning to recognize the importance of energy conservation. Naturally he would never admit that *his* performance is falling off in any way; it's you, poor old soul, who have to be nursed along to a proper state of readiness.

This demands something that is foreign to Willie's generous nature. Never one to discriminate, he has always believed in living according to the law of first come, first served, hating to deprive anyone of the chance of getting to know him. Like a pint-sized Parliamentary candidate, he will press the flesh with all who cross his path, confident in the belief that to know him is to love him.

Those days, due to circumstances beyond his control, are over. But (yet another example of life being unfair) promising opportunities still occur. Women of all ages will happily sit on an old man's lap, tickle his whiskers and generally behave in a friendly and provocative fashion. They think that he's harmless, but he's not. And when Willie rises to the occasion, you can cut the startled atmosphere with a knife.

What these ladies don't realize is that old Willie never dies; he simply bides his time. Even at the very threshold of eternity the sight of a state registered nurse bending over can lead to an upright farewell and an impressive case of rigor mortis. As his friends and admirers would say: *'He died as he had lived.'*

THE DAY OF RECKONING

Miss Hoskins   Good grief! You're not letting him in here, are you?

St Peter   Well, boys will be boys, my dear.

Meanwhile, Willie has been taking a long and appreciative look at Miss Hoskins' legs. The rest of her isn't too bad, either.

Hey – who'd have guessed Heaven and Hell would turn out to be the same place ?!

Nine a.m. Tuesday morning, at the Pearly Gates. St Peter is looking through the book in astonishment.

St Peter   This is indeed a catalogue of vice and mischief. I can't believe it. But perhaps my eyes deceive me. Miss Hoskins, where are my glasses?

Miss Hoskins, who is St Peter's secretary, appears. She has a stern expression, but sensational legs. She looks over St Peter's shoulder at the book.

Willie   We're in luck. This looks like heaven.

Miss Hoskins   None of your nonsense. You're in enough trouble already.

Willie   But those legs! They're to die over.

Miss Hoskins   Too late.

Willie   No, honestly. Tell me, what time do you get off work?

Miss Hoskins   In a couple of billion years.

Willie   Great. I'll be waiting outside in a taxi.

And so on.